Enhancing the Journey:
The Journey Journal

Yvette Wilson Bentley

Enhancing the Journey

Copyright © 2012 Yvette Wilson Bentley

All rights reserved. Except for use in the case of brief quotations embodied in critical articles and reviews, the reproduction or utilization of this work in whole or part in any form by any electronic, digital, mechanical or other means, now known or hereafter invented, including xerography, photocopying, scanning, recording, or any information storage or retrieval system, is forbidden without prior written permission of the author and publisher.

The scanning, uploading, and distribution of this book via the Internet or via any other means without permission of the publisher and author is illegal and punishable by law. Purchase only authorized versions of this book and do not participate in or encourage electronic piracy of copyrighted materials. Your support of the author's rights is appreciated.

For ordering, booking, permission, or questions, contact the author.

ISBN-13: 978-0-9961327-1-8
ISBN-10: 0996132716
Library of Congress Control Number: 2015907083

Fourth Edition
Published by Wryte Type Publishing, LLC
Printed in the United States of America

Enhancing the Journey

DEDICATION

I dedicate this book to the memory of my sister-friend, Dorothy "Jeannie" Palmer, who may be gone from this earth, but I will always carry you in my heart and spirit! THANK YOU for making a difference in my life.

I would like to also dedicate this book to all those who purchased the first edition of my first book and making the year 2012 a commemorative one for me as a new author! Your love and support is priceless!

May you continue to be blessed on your journey!

TABLE OF CONTENTS

Joy in Your Noise	10
What Are You Looking For?	12
Ceaseless Chances	14
Used Without Permission	16
Being Right is Easier than Being Perfect	18
Not In the Water	20
Can You Hear Me?	22
The Nerve of Me!	26
Keep That Appointment	28
Safe Place	31
Knocking On My Own Door	33
Not My Own Understanding	35
The Greatest Job	37

What Did You Eat Today?	39
Making the Time Count	41
Asking Is Not Enough	43
A Worthless Invitation	46
The News Reporter	48
Is My Hand Worth Lending?	51
Truth Without the Trash	53
Rejection to Revelation	55
The Best Gets Better	58
The Love I Never Knew	60
Simple Faith	63
While You're Waiting...	65
The Purpose of Quality	67
No Failure in Trying	69
Respecting Authority	71
New Habits	73
Open the Door	75

Help Me to Forgive Me	77
Don't Just Wake Up……Get Up!	80
The Gift of Discovery	82
God's Validation Is All I Need	84
Grace Is Not a Given…It's a Gift	89
Finding Your Faith	92
No Hiding Place	94
Yes We Can!	98
Come Out of the Quicksand	101
Who's In Charge?	104
What You Think About Me	107
A New Challenge	110
Follow the Instructions	113
Prayer is Not Magical	116
Too Tight	119
No More Fighting	122
Break Free	125

Great Accomplishments	**128**
About the Author	**132**

Joy in Your Noise

Noise is a normal part of life. Whether it's joyous occasions, attending sporting events, birthday parties, holiday events, or just spending time with family and friends, there is a share of noise involved. At a sporting event, I join the crowd in cheering on the winning team and I am usually singing and clapping at a concert. I have been surrounded with the noise, I contributed to the noise, and I had joy in my noise simply because I was happy to be participating in the noise.

Reflecting on activities where I have been a noisy participant, I asked myself, "Am I willing to make noise for God?" And if so, will my noise have joy? At church, do I sing and praise God with joy or am I simply trying to be seen?

Making a joyful noise for God is the best kind of noise I can make, especially when I am worshipping with other believers. If I express just a portion of joy in my noise for God as I do in other areas of my life, I will receive God's power in being blessed and being a blessing to others.

Is there joy in your noise?

What Are You Looking For?

What are you looking for out of life? My grandmother once asked me. "I want a nice car, a nice house, a good job, and plenty of money," was my response. She started laughing and when I asked her why she was laughing, she continued to laugh, which made me angry. What was wrong with the answer I had given her? After all, I couldn't see how to enjoy life any other way, especially being in my early 20s at the time. I discovered that I couldn't obtain or maintain these things.

I had convinced myself that hard work was the only requirement to have what I wanted in life. One of my parents' and grandparents' favorite sayings was to "seek God first." I was convinced that did not apply to me, but I found out later in life that indeed it does apply to me.

I came to accept that God and God alone has all power.

I also accepted that to have success in my life, I need to "seek God first" and the rest will fall into place according to His will, not Yvette's!

Once I began seeking God first in all things, I have experienced successes that I couldn't dream of! Those things I was looking for in my 20's brought physical comfort and pleasure, but true comfort and pleasure manifests in my life when I.......

...look for God first in all things!

Ceaseless Chances

How many times have you had one chance to either do something right or kiss that opportunity goodbye if you did it wrong? On the average job, disciplinary steps consist of a verbal warning, a written warning, a suspension, and then termination from the position. Would you either sympathize or empathize with a person who lost their job, or would you say, "Well, they had their chance and they blew it?" I have taken both of these positions in times past.

Where would I be if God had taken the same attitude towards me? Would I still be here if God gave me a few chances and then cut me off if I didn't get it right the first time? Probably not!

If God allowed me only one chance to get it

right, I would have been spiritually dead long ago. Where would I be if it were not for His grace and mercy that does not cease?

Due to His grace and mercy, my spirit is alive and vibrant. I am no longer a dead woman walking through life. Why does He give me so many chances? I believe part of it is His agape love for me which gives me far more opportunities to get it right than I could ever deserve!

I can't count all the times that He has forgiven me or all the times that His grace and mercy has seen me through, especially when I have made decisions and taken actions that have either sidetracked me or knocked me completely off the track.

God, thank You for your ceaseless chances!

Used Without Permission

Spiritual fitness is essential to be used by God for His purpose and to be of service to my fellow man. When I am willing to be used by God, it is indeed a privilege and the possibilities are endless. I have also found out that God has used me at times to perform His will and I didn't have a clue until after the fact.

I have been guilty of starting out to harm others and then God took over and used me for His good. Despite my numerous attempts to either do what I wanted or treat people how I wanted to, God has intervened and changed my intentions as well as my actions.

In turn, I have encountered people who have done their best to harm me and witnessed God use those very persons to protect me and even elevate me. Of course, I don't see it that way in the midst of a situation; nevertheless, God shows me that regardless of my actions or the actions of others, it is He who is in control! A friend once said, "God will make a liar tell the truth at least one time," just as another friend has said "What the devil means for bad, God means it for your good!" I have been blessed to witness both of these accounts at different times in my life.

To be used by other people for selfish and personal gain is not a great thing. But to be used by God.....what a privilege!

When I accept that God will use me any way He chooses, I can stand in readiness to be used for His will and His glory...

...at any given moment!

Being Right is Easier than Being Perfect

I would love to say that I never bought into the philosophy of being a perfectionist, but that would be untrue. I crowned myself as a perfectionist, especially since I had accomplished things without mistakes or flaws – at least in my opinion!

God revealed to me that HE is the only perfectionist that exists and that His perfect gifts are demonstrated through His Son and the Holy Spirit! Wow! I had spent half of my life trying to be perfect, only to find that it is humanly impossible.

I read a passage that spoke of "spiritual progress rather than spiritual perfection." I realized human perfection does not exist! I had been trying to walk in shoes that I could never fill because I was trying to be "perfect."

Working daily to do what's right is much simpler than working to be perfect. I am not always 100% right and it's OK not to always be 100% right! Human perfection allows no room for flexibility; but striving to do the right thing allows flexibility to make mistakes, learn from those mistakes, and to choose new actions to do the right thing.

It's easier to do the possible right than the impossible perfect!

Not In the Water

I once joined a church and was scheduled to be baptized, but I wanted to go to a concert the same evening. What do I do? As much as I wanted to go to that concert, I didn't want to pass up a chance to "get right with Christ," so I was baptized that evening.

"I have been changed! I will never be the same! I'm a Christian now!" This was what I thought when I came out of the baptismal pool. I started doing what I thought "good" Christians do. I went to church. I went to Sunday School. When church was over, I would drink alcohol, use drugs, have sex, and display other inappropriate behaviors.

Rededicating my life to Christ years later showed me that my past decisions were contrary to trying to live a Christian life.

Being a Christian meant more than going to church for a few hours a week; it meant incorporating what I learned on Sundays into my daily routine, and not when it was convenient for me.

The water is symbol of baptism, but true baptism comes by the baptism of the Holy Spirit. My heart and mind must be open to receive the Holy Spirit in order to receive God's divine direction.

*Baptism in the water
is just the beginning.*

Can You Hear Me?

I stayed in trouble as a child because I was always talking and never listening. After all, I thought I had worthwhile things to say and was an authority on most subjects. My mother used to say, "You talk too much and you would save yourself from a lot of problems if you would learn to shut your mouth and listen!" What did she know?

I simply refused to listen. I thought I knew more than most people most of the time and even when it was obvious they knew more than I did, I still had a voice in the matter. Besides, people told me how smart and intelligent I was, so I nominated myself to be that authoritative voice and listening wasn't necessary.

I have to admit that my mother was right – I would have avoided many problems had listened first. She would remind me of a scripture that says to be "quick to listen and slow to speak," but I looked at her as being old and what she was saying did not apply to me!

About 16 years ago, I joined a life-changing society and every time I went to a gathering, I was running my mouth without fail! After a few months, one of the older members got fed up and told me to "Shut up, just shut up! You can't hear nothing if you're always talking!" Who did he think he was talking to? I'm a grown woman! I muttered a few choice words under my breath, but trust me, under my breath was as far as the words went!

Two years later God revealed to me that I couldn't hear His voice because I would not shut up long enough to listen. He also showed me that He had sent many people to me to give me a word of encouragement, instruction, affirmation, or confirmation, and I had missed out on many opportunities because I would not stop talking long enough to listen to what He was saying to me. Eventually, I thanked that member for telling me to shut up and thanked God for the humility to do so. . Little did I know that God was preparing me to receive an even greater gift....

I was sitting at my mother's kitchen table as she and some of her friends were conversing. For once, I just sat and listened. When my mother realized I was sitting there silent, she said, "You mean that you don't have something to say, Miss Yvette?" With the biggest smile on my face, I replied, "You can't hear nothing if you're always talking." She looked at me and said, "Well I'll be! I think that you finally got it! I've only been trying to teach you that for the last 40 years!"

I thank God every day that my mother witnessed my willingness to talk less and listen more before He called her home to Glory!

Can you hear Me?
Yes, God, I am listening!

The Nerve of Me!

One of my favorite stories in the Bible is the story of Jesus having the Last Supper with the disciples. As remarkable as this story is, it is saddening to read that Peter denied Jesus three times, just as Jesus prophesized that he would. I can remember saying to myself many times, how could Peter deny Jesus? The nerve of him! Then I heard a small voice say, "Well what about you? How many times have you denied Jesus?"

I had to admit that I have denied Jesus more times than I can count. I had shown no regard for the love I claimed to have for God and no acknowledgment of Him as the head of my life! I had a whole lot of nerve judging Peter's actions, especially since mine had not been any better.

I am so grateful to know that God has not rendered the same judgment on me that I have rendered on others! I would be in a world of trouble! I am thankful that God has seen fit to use me for His purpose, even when I denied who He is in my life!

It's a good thing that God's name is God and not Yvette!

Keep That Appointment

Sometimes it is necessary to schedule appointments to balance various life obligations and responsibilities. I have to schedule an appointment to see the doctor or the dentist, just as I have to make an appointment at the hair salon. Then there are other scheduled tasks, such going to work, taking medicine, etc.

I make every effort to arrive early for appointments. For example, I want to arrive at a doctor's appointment early to fill out paperwork, or better yet, I like getting to work a few minutes early to get coffee, use the restroom, etc. before beginning my shift.

In today's world, there are many tools and devices to manage a schedule and appointments

– electronic calendars via cell phones, iPads, PCs, etc. Then there are those who (like me) prefer paper-to-pen methods such as using a good old-fashioned paper calendar.

I devote a considerable amount of time prioritizing tasks and balancing my schedule.

One day, as I was reviewing my schedule, it dawned on me that I failed to schedule a daily appointment with the most important person in my life and that is God!

True enough, I can schedule to meet with God anytime, for He is available 24/7 and His door is always open. Do I always devote a portion of my day to pencil in time with God? No, I don't. Sometimes, the day has come and gone and I realize not only did I not meet with God but I didn't take the time to put Him in my schedule!

Because of God's love for the world, He took the time to give His only begotten son so that people like me can have everlasting life. If He had not placed me in His schedule, where would I be?

When I schedule God as my first appointment

of the day, I am starting my day right, and by keeping that appointment, I receive all I need to make it through the day, regardless of what I may be faced with.

*Make and keep an appointment
with God today!*

Safe Place

In the city where I grew up, the different YMCA branches used to be designated as "safe places" for teenagers. Each of these buildings had a triangular logo of an adult holding a child's hand. If a teenager felt they were in danger, whatever the reason, they could go to a safe place for food, shelter, and physical safety from their traumatic circumstances.

My "safe places" were at home with my mother, my grandmother's house, and with other family friends. I didn't worry about harm or danger because I knew that I would be protected in any of my "safe places."

When I started my spiritual journey, I started

understanding that a "safe place" represents more than physical safety. When I look back over some of my life's events, I have been physically safe; however, I was in spiritual danger. When I was ready to seek refuge, I asked, "What must I "do to be saved?" God immediately granted me a SAFE PLACE in His presence, which is full of His love, His forgiveness, His grace, and His mercy.

When I feel physically safe, I stick close to the environment where I feel safe and protected. Every now and then, I try to put on my "big girl panties" and strike out on my own; however, I don't stray too far or too long. The same applies to my spiritual life! God's grace protects me and keeps me safe in ALL circumstances, so I strive not to stray too far or too long from His presence.

Thank you, God, for giving me a safe place!

Knocking On My Own Door

Watching cartoons and eating breakfast on a Saturday morning was the norm at my house. Meanwhile, my mother would be busy around the house – cleaning, cooking, sewing, and talking on the phone. Then there would be an unexpected knock at the door. I would often go to the top of the stairs and peek as my mother opened the door. There would usually be two to three people, dressed very nicely, and they would talk about how God loved everyone and how He would save my mother and her children. They also left literature and invited her to attend services at their church.

When I think about those "Saturday morning visitors," who came weekly, I can appreciate their confidence and their commitment to witness to others about their beliefs.

On several occasions, a group of my church members got together to do some "door-to-door witnessing" in the church's neighborhood. I was unable to attend, but hearing about the experience, I was left with some things to think about. A member shared that after the group went out into the neighborhood, she found the need to do a "self- door-to-door witnessing."

I contemplated how easy is for me to witness to others about the love of God; yet, there are times when I don't always apply what I know to my own life or circumstances.

Today I have no problem telling anyone what God has done for me, but every now and then, ...

...I need to knock on my own door!

Not My Own Understanding

"I understand." This was my usual response whenever someone would share information with me. I claimed to understand many things only to find out that I didn't have a clue. Either I didn't have all the information or I was unable to relate due to lack of experience. There were times when I acted based on what I thought I understood only to find myself back to square one, simply because I didn't have enough information or experience.

"Yvette, there are some things that are not meant for you to understand," my mother once told me. Once again, I know that she was right about it. My understanding has either taken me places I didn't want to go or had no business going in the first place! If I had the capacity to understand all things, then I would have no need for God's direction.

The Word of God instructs us not to "lean on our own understanding." Having daily communication with God enhances my understanding with the things that He has designed for me to understand.

To fully understand all things is humanly impossible; however, the simple solution for me is to trust God for the understanding that He deems for me to have.

*God hasn't led me down
the wrong path yet!*

The Greatest Job

About two years ago, I lost my job. "What am I going to do?" "How am I going to make it?" Fear began to set in, job opportunities were scarce, and resources were slim. I began praying about my situation and at first I wasn't feeling any relief, then one day, God reminded me of my job responsibilities as a Christian – serve Him and serve others.

I spent my time being of service at my church and helping others in the community. "Lord, I know you are going to make a way. I don't know how, but I know you are and I trust you to do it." I still had the fear, but it wasn't as intense when I kept myself busy. A friend told me, "God is keeping you busy while He is working it out and stay out of His business!"

Three weeks later, I found out my unemployment claim had been denied. "What am I going to do, God?" I then asked, "God I believe that you are working it out, but can you please show me a sign?"! God is so amazing – He heard my cry and three hours later, I received a job offer!

As I was preparing for the new job, I realized this job would meet my earthly needs; however, I already had a job - to follow God, live by His Word, and to tell others the Good News!

The new job came with benefits, but working for God comes with guarantees: no unemployment, no demotions, and the salary of everlasting life!

How can I turn down a job like that?

What Did You Eat Today?

"What did you eat today?" My answer would vary from what day it was to my state of mind that particular day. One day may be a steak dinner, the next day may be a fried chicken dinner, then other days it may be a peanut butter & jelly sandwich. Most days, I eat at least two meals and one or two snacks but whatever I eat normally satisfies my appetite.

Just as I have to feed my physical body, I have to also feed my spirit and after some self-examination, I found that I get "fed" the Word of God every time I attend church or Bible study, but outside of that, I was spiritually hungry, and even had moments of suffering from spiritual starvation.

How did I know I was spiritually starving? Because I was not partaking in God's Word on a daily basis!

According to God's Word, we are to ask Him for our "daily bread" for spiritual nourishment. I have heard the reference of "our daily bread" most of my life, but the part that I had always missed was that this was something that I am supposed to do each day! Where do I find "our daily bread?" The Word will cure those spiritual "hunger pangs" every time!

Is your spirit hungry?
What did you eat today?

Making the Time Count

I once was assigned a special project at work that was in addition to my regular job duties. My first step in mapping out a plan to complete the task was to find out how much time I had to complete it. Then, I scheduled a set number of hours daily to meet the deadline; however, I didn't meet the deadline and I had to explain that to my supervisor. I gave him an explanation; he reviewed my work, and gave me feedback that surprised me. He told me that the work that I had done thus far had exceeded his expectations and decided to extend the deadline.

At first, I was disappointed in myself for not meeting the deadline but I found inspiration in my supervisor's feedback. I met the new deadline, and the project was a huge success!

God has given me time to do certain things and I have taken much of that time for granted by not abiding by His will for me. Thank God for his grace and mercy! Just as my supervisor gave me more time to finish that project, God has given me more time to get some things right, despite the time that I have wasted.

I don't take time for granted today. I can't count the time I have left on this earth, but with God's help, I may not always count my time accurately, but I do my very best to...

...make my time count!

Asking Is Not Enough

I have experienced pain in many forms. Some pain has been through the actions of others just as I have experienced pain through self-infliction. Whenever I found myself in pain, my first thought would be how to make the pain go away. I used to try my own methods, and after I saw that my methods were not working, I started learning how to seek God for relief.

I remember one instance asking God to take my pain away but the pain would not leave. I believed God could take the pain away. I had heard many testimonies of how God was delivering people from their pain, but I began to wonder why God was allowing me to stay in pain because I had pleaded with Him but the relief was not there, at least not yet!

I once heard a lady at church testify about her husband physically abusing her. She said that for years she asked God to take away the pain of the beatings. One day, she decided to leave her husband and her relief came once she was willing to remove herself from the source of her pain - at home with her husband.

I went home and asked myself, "Is asking Him to take the pain away not enough?" When I looked back over past painful situations, the answer came: NO, asking was not enough. I believe that God was waiting for me to do my part, which was to let go of the source of the pain – that person, place, thing, or situation – and once I let go, then He gave me the relief that I had been seeking.

God doesn't need my help, but when I make the effort without always looking for Him to do for me what I can do for myself, He shows up and shows out every time! I seek God often for deliverance and He continues to show me that although He doesn't need my help, my participation in my own deliverance is necessary. Asking Him is not enough!

*God, please show me
the actions to take!*

A Worthless Invitation

I once invited some friends over for Thanksgiving Dinner. I had invited one friend and completely ignored her. I was so busy entertaining other guests that I disregarded her presence. When it was time to bless the food, I looked around and the person had left. I called her but my calls went unanswered. I had great time with my other guests, but I could not understand why she left without saying a word.

The next day, this person called and when I asked why she left, she told me that I had invited her to my home but I didn't make her feel welcomed. "If you weren't welcomed, I would have never invited you," I replied. She then disconnected the call. I thought about that call throughout the day and realized that she was right – I had not made her feel welcomed. I had totally ignored her presence. If it were not for my actions, the outcome may have been different.

When I was invited to join my current church, the members also welcomed me. Not once do I recall being ignored or feeling unwelcomed and the warm welcome that I received over two years ago has remained constant – it is as warm and friendly today as it was in the beginning.

I learned a valuable lesson from that Thanksgiving Day dinner: the same welcome that I look to receive is the same welcome that I should give!

There's more to an invitation
that just an invite!

The News Reporter

The evening TV news comes on at least twice daily. When I was young, the times were at 6 p.m. and at 11 p.m. I was usually asleep before 11 p.m. but I was always in front of the TV when the 6 p.m. news came on. My favorite part of the newscast was to hear the reporters say, "In the news..." and then they would report the current events, the weather, sports, etc.

As a young woman, I prided myself on being "in the know" and I would not hesitate to report the news of what was going on – whether it was about me or others; whether it was good or bad. I didn't always have all the facts; sometimes I didn't have a clue of what I was talking about; nonetheless, it didn't stop me from telling the news.

Sitting in a Sunday School class, the teacher mentioned that Christians are responsible for telling the Good News! I had heard that before, but now the statement caught my attention. I used to think that telling the Good News was complicated and that I was not qualified to do such a thing. At different times, I wanted to ask, "What does it mean to tell the Good News?" but for fear of appearing ignorant, I would convince myself not to ask. Just as I was thinking about this, the teacher said, "What does it mean to tell the Good News? It simply means to tell your story of what God has done in your life."

I had wanted to know the answer to that question for years but fear would stop me from asking. I was relieved to find that the answer was simple ...tell others what God has done in my life! I can that story at any time, any place, and to anyone that is willing to listen. Not a complicated task at all!

Thank you, God, for allowing me to bear the Good News!

Is My Hand Worth Lending?

"Lend a helping hand" is a familiar phrase as far back as I can remember. As a little girl, I was taught to always help others. I have witnessed fine examples of people helping others as if it were second nature to them.

Helping others has become more prevalent to me over the years but before I extend my hand to someone, I have to look at my intentions: Will I pull them up or push them down? Am I looking to give or to gain? Will I ask others to assist me if I am unable to do it alone? Last, but not least, am I seeking God for strength or am I operating on own devices?

With the greatest intentions, I may do a

person or a situation more harm than good by offering my help. This is when I have to seek God and ask Him for His direction whether or not to offer my assistance. Sometimes He says yes; other times He may say no. God knows better than I when I am capable of lending a helping hand!

My job is to be ready
when He does say YES!

Truth Without the Trash

I know that I have a responsibility to tell the Good News of what God has done in my life, but I'm not always comfortable in doing so, especially when I have to give accounts of past actions that are unpleasant and I'm not very proud of.

When speaking with others, I try not to speak in such a way that people don't understand what I am saying. But at the same time, I don't want to use vulgar or profane language to illustrate a point that will offend people and diminish my purpose. I do believe in being honest. A friend once told me, "Honesty without compassion is pure hostility," and I don't want to be perceived as a hostile person by using inappropriate language.

God has shown me that I can be truthful without using "trashy" language and tell the Good News with dignity and taste, which shows respect to others and to me.

> *Thank God for taking the*
> *trash out of my truth!*

Rejection to Revelation

I once met a person and we became instant friends. We had a lot in common and shared many of the same spiritual beliefs. I regarded her as an "extended family member" and made it known to her that whatever went down the pipe, I had her back! With this friend, I shared my time and my resources, even at the risk of putting their needs above my own. After some time, I would call my friend, but my calls went unanswered. I would leave multiple messages with no response. What happened? We were supposed to have each other's back! Why were they rejecting me? All I knew at the moment was that this hurts!

After praying and searching myself, I was

faced with some hard facts. I was initiating the majority of our communications. I was glad to volunteer my time and resources, but I found that

I had placed an expectation and then became angry when it was not being reciprocated. In short, I was people-pleasing and I placed myself in a position to be used up and then discarded by this person.

I asked God, "If I am supposed to help people, then why am I hurting behind it? How do I prevent that?" God said to me, "Quit seeking people to help and allow Me to show you who to help."

I began to experience a transformation. It is more important for me to glorify God in helping people rather than looking for people to accept me based on my expectations. What I know today is that if God isn't in it, it just won't work!

The painful experience with that person turned out to be God preparing me for new and positive experiences in friendships. The rejection that I felt proved to be a revelation – God used that situation to make room for the people that He intended to bring into my life which would complement His will and purpose for my present and future life.

*Rejection isn't always
a bad thing!*

The Best Gets Better

Sometimes my mother would tell me to do things but I wouldn't always do whatever it was she expected me to do. Whenever that occurred, I would be quick to tell her, "Well I am doing the best that I can," but with my mother, that excuse did not work. She wasn't having it! She would then remind me of exactly what I need to do to get it right, but I wouldn't always put forth the extra effort, and I would find myself back "in the doghouse" until I did exactly what she told me to do.

I have been guilty of half-stepping with my actions and not giving my best performance, even when I had said that I had. There were times where my attitude has been, "I've done my best and I'm not doing anything extra. That's it and that's all!" Not the best attitude to have, is it?

When I operate on my own thinking to believe that I have done my best, I limit myself. However, when I rely on God, He encourages me to "go the extra mile," which makes my best a little better. Where I am limited, God's power is unlimited.

When I embrace more of God's power and less of my own, my best gets better!

The Love I Never Knew

"You have to learn to love yourself." When I would hear that, I would laugh, and then say to myself, "I love myself and can't imagine not loving myself." After all, I thought, how can anyone not love themselves?

I loved myself; after all, I was that girl. I had my stuff together, didn't allow most things to bother me, and when all else failed, God would carry me through. I truly believed this about myself until I looked at my actions and realized that I was only fooling myself about my love for self.

I was forced to ask myself, "Do you really love yourself?" "Where was the love for myself when I was drinking alcohol, using drugs, going along to get along, going to jail, depending on others to do for me what I could do for myself, and acting as if I didn't know the difference between right and wrong?" For years, I had convinced of being that girl, only to find that I was a dressed up garbage can!

I was clueless about self-love. With all that I thought I had and all that I thought I was, nobody could have ever told me that I didn't love myself, but it's difficult to escape the truth when it is staring you straight in the face! The evidence of my life spoke for itself.

Someone told me, "When you quit looking for something or someone outside of yourself to fill God's place in your heart, you will discover the love for self."

I invited God into my heart and found out that God is love! Once I began experiencing the love of God, my life has never been the same.

God's love strengthens me to "love me some me!"

Simple Faith

I have heard people testify about their faith in God. I used to think, "I want to have faith in God, but I don't know how!" I truly believed this and had convinced myself I would never be able to achieve it.

I was having a conversation with a person and they brought up the subject of having faith in God. At first I wanted to shut down because I could not see myself capable of having the faith that I have heard so many people talk about. But then the person gave me an illustration that proved to be very practical. They said, "Look at the chair that you're sitting in. As you prepared to sit in that chair, didn't you believe that you could sit in that chair without falling down?" I answered "yes". They asked me why I said "yes" and my response was because it has four legs to support me when I sit down. The person began to laugh and then said, "Well, Yvette, that is a pure example of faith – you didn't know if the chair would support you, but you believed that it would; therefore, you had faith that it would."

That conversation left a huge impression on me and left me with this revelation: Just as I had faith that the chair would support me, I can have the same faith in God. All I have to do is believe! I have possessed the power of faith, but it was after that conversation that I realized to have faith in God is to use a power I've always had – the power to believe!

To have faith is to believe.
It's just that simple!

While You're Waiting...

"God has a purpose for your life!" I would hear it from my mother, my father, my grandmother, my school teachers, and a few others. I used to blow it off when I heard it because I knew what I wanted my purpose in life to be and it was my decision and my decision alone!

I have been exposed to various opportunities and experiences and regarded myself as a "multi-talented" individual and I had some choices to define my own purpose. Some of the things that I thought would work didn't work where others didn't give me the fulfillment of purpose that I thought they would. God has allowed me to be good at a few things. After experiencing trials and errors, I began to wonder what it is I am supposed to be doing. I didn't doubt that I had a purpose but I had to admit at that moment, I didn't have a clue of what my purpose was supposed to be.

I met with my pastor and asked him, "God seems to reveal to others what their purpose is; why is He taking so long to reveal mine to me?" He told me that God will reveal my purpose to me in His time. That confused me at first, but then my pastor advised that, "While you're waiting for God to reveals your purpose, continue to do the next right things, such as serve God, serve others, go to work, pay your bills, etc."

When God reveals my purpose to me
in His time is when it will be THE TIME!

The Purpose of Quality

I had a fish aquarium in my work office and decided to purchase some goldfish. I figured the fish would bring a relaxing and calming feel to the office atmosphere, so my co-worker and I were excited once we filled the tank with water and started watching the fish swim around.

In a few weeks, all the fish died, except for one. The next day I noticed something unique about that one fish – he had only one eye! I hadn't thought about giving names to the fish, but when I looked at the lone survivor, I named him TRUDGE. To "trudge" means to have purpose, and it was obvious that this lone fish with one eye had a purpose to fulfill.

Trudge grew to a pretty good size and continued to swim through the aquarium. I thought about getting more fish, but decided against it for two reasons: One, Trudge seemed pretty content swimming around alone, and two, he served my purpose for buying the fish in the first place, which was to bring a relaxing and calming feel to the office atmosphere. Trudge's life in my aquarium represented a life with quality. What I expected from six goldfish was carried out successfully by one goldfish with one eye!

There is more significance in one thing with the quality of completion than the quantity of incompletion represented by two or more things.

Quantity, in this case, proved to be irrelevant.

Quality serves a greater purpose than quantity!

No Failure in Trying

I once lost a job after and it was a loss to me in two ways. First, losing the job, and second, the feelings that I experienced - anger, hurt, rejection - but most of all, failure. I felt that I had not only failed at the job, but I had failed myself. A friend told me that it was dangerous to think of myself as a failure. When I asked her why she they made that statement, she simply told me to seek God for the answer.

God showed me that by considering myself a failure, I was allowing failure to determine my fate, and until I changed my perception, nothing would change. But if I changed my perception from being a failure to experiencing a loss, then I can be opened to follow God's guidance to change my fate rather than to finalize it through failure.

God reminded me that I was not a failure and when I asked him what should I do, the answer was simple ...try!

> *After all, the only thing to*
> *beat a failure is a try!*

Respecting Authority

From childhood, I have been taught to respect others. I was taught to address adults with "Yes ma'am," "No ma'am," "Yes sir," and "No sir." I was also not allowed to call adults by their first names – it was always "Miss" or "Mister." If I wanted to do something, then I had to ask an adult's permission and then abide by their decision, which usually was either YES or NO!

Being disrespectful was not an option; I was required to show respect at all times. Was I respectful at all times? No I wasn't, and please believe, my parents and other adults had no problem giving me consequences to remind me of what I was supposed to be – respectful at all times!

I strive daily in giving God the highest respect as my Heavenly Father. I need to ask for His permission before doing things on my own. I would have avoided many consequences had I shown God the respect that He deserves by asking for permission before taking matters into my own hands. Just as my daddy may have told me yes or no regarding certain things, my Heavenly Father does the same and I need to be respectful of that at all times!

When I am willing to respect authority, some consequences are avoidable!

New Habits

One day I thought about a few of my daily habits, like drinking coffee, watching the news, talking on the phone, etc. Then I gave some thought to other habits, which are too many to count. I found just as I have positive habits, I also have negative habits. There are some I need to keep, some I need to be rid of, and then there are others that I need to add.

My habits, both good and bad, have one thing in common – they became habits because I took an interest in each one. I either took an interest in learning how to make them work for me, or else I took an interest in trying to make them work for me, even when they didn't work. I have prospered with positive habits, just as I have endured pain with negative habits.

Growing in God and receiving the benefits requires new habits, such as prayer, meditation, studying the Word, fellowship, and service. I am no stranger to these habits; however, they did not begin to work for me until I took an interest in developing them. Practicing habits can either bring prosperity or pain to your life.

I want to practice prospering habits!

Open the Door

"It's just me against the world." At one time, that was the design of my life. Despite family and friends that cared about me, I perceived myself as a misunderstood individual and when it was all said and done, I was all by myself and all alone.

I had bottled up heartaches and pain that I wouldn't share with anyone. Either nobody cared or they would just hurt me more. My solution would be to self-medicate and further barricade myself in my pain.

I was going to explode if I didn't quickly do something different! All my efforts had failed and I had one alternative – to turn to God. My mother even told me to turn to God. It took some time and willingness to do that. After all, God knew all that was going on with me, so why did I have to tell Him things that He already knew?

"When the pain gets great enough, you will do something different."

I cried out to God and asked Him to help me. He showed me that if I would open the door, He would send me the help that I need. And that He did!

Are you tired of hurting and suffering? Just open the door for God!

He's waiting!

Help Me to Forgive Me

During my thirty-something years, I decided to do something that I thought was beneficial to me. A few months later, I was left devastated, in tremendous pain, and on the verge of spiritual bankruptcy, which were the by-products of the decision that I had made. I had thoughts of "throwing in the towel" and giving up on having any happiness. Fortunately, I had a moment of clarity and decided to ask for help.

I met with an associate minister at my church. She listened patiently as I shared my problems and how I believed I had been defeated by these problems all due to the decision that I had made. I told her that I had cried out to God, but I wasn't getting any relief.

The minister then asked me: "How soon do you think God forgives you when you ask for forgiveness?" I sat straight up and said, "As soon as you ask," was my reply. She sat there for a moment and then said, "Well, Yvette, if God forgives you as soon as you ask, then what is taking you so long to forgive yourself?" As I began to cry, I thanked God for His forgiveness asked Him to help me forgive myself. The minister prayed with me and after that prayer, I realized that relief had finally arrived!

I had been holding myself in bondage simply because I had not forgiven myself. When I procrastinate in forgiving myself, I leave the door open for that "lower power" to convince me I am not worthy of God's forgiveness or my own. If I wanted freedom from the bondage, then I had to forgive myself, which is exactly what I did at that moment!

I left that meeting full of relief, gratitude, and a new perception. I have made my share of mistakes and will make plenty more in this lifetime, but with the grace and mercy of a loving

God, I take comfort in knowing that He loves me so much that He will forgive me of my sins as soon as I ask, which proves to me that I don't have to take all day in forgiving myself!

God teaches me to love myself so
I can forgive myself!

Don't Just Wake Up......Get Up!

I have watched movies that had characters that would sleepwalk. I would laugh at the things they would do while they were sleepwalking, and would laugh even more once they woke up and couldn't recall any of their actions or conversations they had while they were sleepwalking.

I can recall a time when I was sleepwalking through life. When my behavior was contradictory to how my parents had raised me, I was sleepwalking. When I refused to heed to certain situations, even when destruction was evident from the beginning, I was sleepwalking. I was on a one-way road, headed for destruction, and was clueless. One day, my mother asked me, "When are you going to wake up?" She doesn't know what's she's talking about, I thought, but once again, I found that she did and something had to change.

"Wake Up Everybody" by Harold Melvin & the Blue Notes (featuring the late Teddy Pendergrass) has been one of my favorite songs since I was a little girl. I would sing and dance whenever I heard it. As I was listening to the song on this particular day, I heard the words, "Wake up, everybody. Get up, get up, everybody!" I started thinking about the conversation with my mother and now I understood why she was telling me to "wake up," but more importantly, it was time to "get up!" The time had come for change. God, please, help me to get up!

*When you wake up and don't
like what you see,
ask God to help you GET UP!!*

The Gift of Discovery

I used to seek out things that I thought would make me happy with my life and I would be a whole person. I sought out material things, pats on the back, social acceptance, professional status, and the love of others and had no problem in going to the extreme in search of obtaining these things.

I would seek out people that I believed needed me, only to be weighed down with resentments either when they no longer needed me or they wouldn't allow me to control them. As much as I hate to admit this, I used to believe that when all else failed, I could use money to get what I or who I wanted in my life. I have a collection of painful experiences that reminds me those methods do not work.

There are things that I may have to look for in life, but then there are things that God has designed for my life that discover and embrace me when He knows that I am ready for them. Sometimes, I am not always ready for what God has for me.

God has great things in store for my life according to His purpose and His timing. Where my timing wants me to hurry up and get to the next level, God's timing advances me to the next level only when He is ready for that to happen and I am mature enough to handle it.

When I allowed God to "take the wheel" and not be so focused on looking for things on my own, what I have found is that I don't even have to look.

When He means for me to have it,
He will allow IT to discover ME!

God's Validation Is All I Need

As I recently completed my first book, I have reflected back over my life and some of the projects that I have taken on. I have been fortunate to complete a few projects in my life; however, I have also been unfortunate in not completing some projects. The truth of the matter is that even though I have completed some things, there are MANY things that I have started on, dropped the ball in the middle of the process, and then the next thing you know I had a pile of different things that I had left undone.

When I would have a numerous of things undone pile up on me, I would beat up on myself with guilt, shame, and failure of not finishing things that I had started. I would convince myself that either, "I was a failure" or either I would ask myself, "What's the use? If I could do it, it would be done!" Then after I would begin to beat myself up pretty good, I would look for other people to validate me in order not to feel what I was feeling. I would seek or expect their validation in order to feel better about myself and when that didn't happen, then once again, the self-beatings would again commence!

Let me share with you about my last experience with my own whipping post. I had mapped out this PERFECT plan of how things were going to go during the process of publishing my first book; however, things didn't go EXACTLY the way that I thought they should have or could have. Before I began whipping myself, I did something that maybe you can relate to.....I declared myself a VICTIM! If THIS hadn't happened, if THAT hadn't happened, if only THEY would do this or if THEY hadn't done that, then my plan would have worked. Well, after that didn't sit well with me, I broke out the whipping post once again. I thank God every day I have a number of people in my life that love me UNCONDITIONALLY, are willing to tell me the TRUTH and "get me all the way together!"

After Bible Study one Wednesday evening, I was whining to one of my church sisters about how MY plan did not come together. After she listened to me whine, she then looked me in the eye and told me to "quit trying to fit my square pegs in the round holes and allow GOD to lead me in fulfilling my plan!" She then went on to tell me that she was not trying to hurt my feelings and that she was giving me some TOUGH LOVE!

Now in times past when someone would attempt to give me TOUGH LOVE, I would do whatever I could do to avoid it. But as we were having this conversation, I realized that her actions were demonstrating a theory that a late friend of mine lived by: "Honesty without compassion is PURE hostility!" She indeed was giving me TOUGH LOVE; however, she was honest, loving, compassionate, and I have no doubt that she came to me in Christian spirit and love!

About two days later, I had a revelation: I was getting in my own way! Not easy to admit, but I found it to be truth. Now it would have been much easier for me to say that others had been getting in my way, but the truth of that is that if they have gotten in my way it is because I have ALLOWED it!

With that being said, I knew it was time for me to stop pointing the BLAME and begin to accept RESPONSIBILITY! I was now faced with a question.....Do I remain the same or do I seek change? I am proud to say that I opted for SEEKING CHANGE!

I was participating on a conference call and the facilitator said that we all have a LIFE ASSGIMENT that God gives us to fulfill and that must be in alignment with Him in order to fulfill the assignment. Then it hit me.....I have been looking for others to VALIDATE who I am and what I do most of my life and not seeking God's validation in this matter!

As a human being, do I need ENCOURAGEMENT and SUPPORT from other human beings? ABSOLUTELY! However, I have to stop SEEKING AND EXPECTING others to validate me!

The ONLY validation that I need to fulfill God's purpose for my life must come from God and ONLY from God! After all, as a Christian, I should continue to strive daily for my thoughts and my actions to be pleasing in His sight, rather than the sight of myself as well as the sight of others!

*God's validation is not only enough,
but it is MORE than enough!*

Grace Is Not a Given…It's a Gift

My life's experiences have produced numerous levels of expectations when it came to getting what I wanted or what I thought I was entitled to. However big or small the expectation was not really important to me as long as they produced the outcome that I desired.

Once I began taking my relationship with God seriously, I believed that I was entitled to receive His grace in my life. After all, God had bestowed His grace upon me many, many times when I was not interested in having a relationship with Him, so now that I have acknowledged a relationship with God, I deserve His grace and I am entitled to it. Wasn't that what being a Christian was all about? I thought so, at least at that time, I did!

While attending a spiritual luncheon for women, I heard the speaker say, "God's JUSTICE is that you get what you deserve, God's MERCY is that you don't get what you deserve, and God's GRACE is that you get better than what you deserve."

Better than what I deserve. Better than what I deserve. Those five words rang in my thoughts over and over again. After several weeks had passed, just when I thought I had escaped those in my thoughts, the message became crystal-clear: God doesn't OWE me anything! He never has owed me anything and He never will owe me anything. God was not obligated to save me from me when I made bad choices and decisions, but He did! God was not obligated to empower me to break the cycle of substance abuse addiction, but He did! God also was not obligated to allow me another chance to be a productive member of society, but He did!

The majority of my life's negative experiences

have been troubles of my own making! I have not said or done anything to deserve God's grace, but because He is so loving, so caring, so generous, and so forgiving, He has given me better than what I deserve on more than one occasion by bestowing upon me the gift of grace!

Today, I have learned that I have no right to expect God's grace in my life – grace is not a given; however, I am responsible for allowing my actions to reflect my appreciation to God for allowing me to be the recipient of such a priceless gift!

Grace is not a given; it's a gift!

Finding Your Faith

Someone once witnessed to me about having faith in God. I wanted to have faith in God, but at the time, I didn't know how and had convinced myself that for me to have faith in God was simply unachievable! A short time later, I was conversing with another person and they brought up the subject of having faith in God. Because I believed faith in God to be unachievable, I started to shut myself completely off from the conversation, but then the person gave me a practical illustration:

"Look at that chair that you're sitting in. As you prepared to sit in that chair, didn't you believe that you could sit in that chair without falling down?" I answered YES. They asked me why I said yes. "It has four legs to support me when I sit down," was my reply. The person began to laugh and then said, "Well, Yvette, that is a pure example of faith, is it not?"

After I thought about that example for a few days, I began to comprehend what that person had shown me. Just as I have faith that the chair will support me, I can exercise that same faith in God keeping me, that is, if I allow Him to!

Thank God for the revelation of faith and thank Him for understanding that faith indeed requires WORK on my part! Like my grandmother used to say, "To whom much is given, much is required."

*If you haven't found your faith yet,
you will find it when you look within yourself!*

No Hiding Place

"I need a break!" "Let me take some days off from work!" "I can't wait to get away!" "I need to get away from everything and everybody!" "Calgon, take me away!" "I just need to go somewhere and exhale!" "Everybody and everything is working my nerves!"

Sound familiar? Can you relate? Not only do they sound familiar and relatable but I have expressed those thoughts in a thousand different ways and at the end of the day, they all shared the common desire of running away to seclude myself from my world as I know it.

Isn't the thought of getting away wonderful?

You come up with the ultimate plan and then

take action. You jump in the car, on a plane, on a boat, or a train.

Once everything has come into play, you inhale a sigh of relief. You may savor the moment of inhaling and then exhaling that relief by closing your eyes just for that moment.

You contemplated your plan and now you are filled with expectations, excitement, and enchantment because you are now executing your plan.

You arrive at your destination. You managed to get away! Yippee! You feel a sense of control and ease! As you settle into your temporary digs, it is with all likelihood there is one thing that hasn't crossed your mind: With the strides you have taken to pull off your "great escape" from everything and everybody, there is ONE person that you can't escape from, regardless of your elaborate plans and the concerted effort to exercise that plan. Are you wondering who that person is? I bet you are!

If you haven't figured it out yet, just take a

look in the mirror. YOU are the only person that you see in the mirror at the moment and YOU are the one person in the world that YOU can't escape from, NOT EVEN FOR A SECOND!

The inability to escape from myself never occurred to me until I heard someone say, "Wherever you go, there you are!" We can escape our families, our friends, our jobs, or even our routine surroundings, but we cannot escape ourselves, nor can we escape our thoughts our feelings, and our emotions that make up the whole self. I am the one person that I have to deal with everywhere I go and in everything I do, but the good news is that help is available when I get to be too much for myself or start working my own nerves!

"God takes care of babies and fools." I have heard that saying all of my life and don't have a clue of its origin, but what I do know is that when I look back over my life, I have indeed made some foolish decisions and certainly demonstrated foolish behavior. No doubt that it is because of

God's grace and mercy I am able to share with others about a few of my former shenanigans and occasionally share a good laugh about them.

I take great release today in knowing that with God in my life, I no longer try to hide from myself. I spent a lot of years and energy trying to achieve the impossible – there's nowhere for me to hide from myself! God gives me the courage to face myself and to accept myself for who I was, who I am, and who I am striving to be!

God, thank you for letting me know that the place for me to hide from myself <u>does not exist</u>!

Yes We Can!

"I know we can make it,
(I know that we can),
I know darn well we can work it out.
Oh yes we can-can, yes we can-can,
why can't we?
If we wanna, yes we can-can!"
(A. Troussaint)

I spent many years trying to live life on my own. I was raised to be a strong and independent person and I thought being strong and independent was all that was required for me to be a success in life. Well, I was wrong about that!

I used to allow my pride to block me off from

asking for help with different things, but after incorporating spiritual principles and guidance into my life, I was able to get to the root of my problem. I was AFRAID! I was AFRAID to ask anyone for help; I was AFRAID that someone knew more than I did. I was AFRAID that I would look small or inadequate because someone knew more than I did, but most of all, I was AFRAID that if I asked for someone's help, they would take my ideas or my dreams away from me!

Whenever I tried to do things on my own, I was practicing and experiencing insanity at its best!

God relieved me from that insanity as soon as I asked Him and my life has taken on a whole new meaning!

Whether it's a new encounter or a familiar experience, it has behooved me to embrace the support of others, which has generated a countless number of wonderful and meaningful experiences. I realized that I do need support and encouragement from others. I cannot live successfully in the world alone. Yes, I am a strong and independent individual; however, when I honestly and truthfully embrace others, I am stronger!

The support of others elevates my knowledge as well as contributes new knowledge in my life each and every day!

What I can't do alone, WE can do together!

Put your hand in mine and together WE can make it!

Yes we CAN!

Come Out of the Quicksand

I had an altercation with a person and was resentful about it for months. Whenever I thought about that person, heard their name, or saw them walk around all happy-go-lucky, my whole demeanor would take a negative shift within about 0.2 seconds!

As I was visiting a friend one day, I began whining about the past altercation. After listening to me, my friend told me that while I was still resentful about the situation, the other person had gone on about their business. She then stated that, "Staying stuck in the past is not going to change what had happened." She's not saying the right things, I thought, but I did hear her out and then left shortly after the conversation.

I have to honestly say I was searching for someone to validate my feelings. Since the first friend was not saying what I wanted to hear, I decided to talk to a second friend. She did not validate my feelings either, but she offered me a suggestion. When I asked her what that was, she said, "It's time to reclaim your power!" "OK, I get it," I said. "I can wreak havoc!" "No," my friend replied, "I said reclaim your power – not hurt someone because you believe they hurt you. Reclaiming your power means to accept the situation, forgive the person, forgive YOURSELF, and move on!"

Talk about a POWERFUL statement! Those three words, reclaim my power, would not leave my thoughts. As long as I allowed that resentment (or any other resentment) to filter into my life, I could not move forward! So I put my "big girl panties on," and exercised the power of acceptance and forgiveness, which ultimately gave me the freedom to move forward. I had reclaimed my power!

Harboring that resentment was just like walking in quicksand –my feet were moving, but I wasn't going anywhere. I thank God that He spoke through a friend to let me know that the power to get out of the quicksand was within reach, if I wanted it.

You don't have to stay stuck.
Reclaim your power and keep it moving!

Who's In Charge?

When I got to be about 13 or 14 years old, I started "smelling myself," a term coined by the older folks of my generation. "Smelling yourself" meant thinking you were grown enough to make your own decisions and do whatever you wanted to do. I was tired of my mother telling me what to do and I felt like that the time had come for me to be in charge of my life. I used to hate to hear my mother say that, "She paid the cost to be the boss and what she said goes."

So I made up my mind that it was time for me to pay the cost to be my own boss and whatever I say goes. I fought my mother on that tooth-and-nail, but once I turned 18 years old, there was no stopping me – I am now in charge of my life!

For the next 13 years, my life was like being on a snowball to hell. Between the people I was involved with, substance abuse, and a few trips to jail, it is only by God's grace that I am still here! For someone who thought they had all the answers, I was clueless!

There's a passage from a book that I familiarized myself with that I remind myself of on a daily basis: "I had to quit playing God; it didn't work!"

God revealed to me that in order for me to make it in this life required willingness to follow His laws and not my own. And if that wasn't

enough, He also told me that now is the time for me to do what He has chosen me to do rather than what I choose to do! I didn't understand exactly what that meant at that moment, but my understanding becomes somewhat clearer each and every day.

Accepting God's charge over my life makes life much simpler for me. Of course, my willingness does not always hit the 100% mark; honestly, sometimes it doesn't hit the mark at all. As I continue on my spiritual journey, God grants me wisdom to know the difference between when He's in charge versus me trying to take charge. I fare much better with God being in charge.

After all, where has being in charge of my own life gotten me?

What You Think About Me

Through my life I have learned that people will say things about you. Sometimes things are said that are not always positive. Remember the old saying, "Don't dish it out if you can't take it?" I had no problem of "dishing it out," but "taking it" was a different story.

When someone told me what they thought of me, especially when they were "telling me off" I would put my hand on my hip, roll my eyes, and say, "I don't care what you think about me." I would make other gestures to demonstrate that I meant what I said - that I don't care what you think and I mean it! Now once I was by myself I had painful and emotional fits behind what had been said to me or about me. As I got older I used different vices to medicate the pain I was feeling because of what people said or thought of me.

It was easy to act like I didn't care in front of others, but deep down inside, I really did care what people thought about me. Why did I care? First of all, I wanted people to like me. Second, I wanted to fit in. Third, I knew that if you were mad at me, then it was a chance that you didn't want to be a part of my life. Whenever I felt like you were going to kick me to the curb, I was willing to do just whatever it took to prevent that. Whatever it took to change your mind, I was willing to do it, only to find myself in more misery when that plan failed me.

I used that statement of "I don't care what you think" as a defense mechanism to camouflage my fear of rejection. I came to believe and accept that I was powerless over what other people think about me. I hated that that feeling of powerlessness but more important, trying to exercise power that I did not have was wearing me out.

After doing some intense work on myself, I gained the power of acceptance which fueled a new perception for me on what people said or thought of me. Do I care what people think of me? Yes, I do. Can I change what people choose to think of me? No I cannot.

The only way that people will change their thinking about me is if they decide to change their thinking. I have no control of what people think of me. My acceptance of these things affords me a new sense of freedom.

*Whatever you think about me is
none of my business!*

A New Challenge

Throughout my life, I have had to face myself and my actions. More times than none, my actions usually backed me into a corner. I would make those promises to myself and to others that I am going to get my life together. With all sincerity, I would have the best of intentions to keep those promises during the moment. Once the moment passed, I may have followed through with changing my actions, but there were many times that I didn't see making a change as an option or a benefit, so I would revert back to actions that were familiar to me.

Thank God, I came to that point in my life where if I didn't start taking things seriously and work on getting my life together, I wouldn't be right here, right now sharing this experience with you!

A huge benefit of striving to live by spiritual principles is that I have a process that helps me to see that there are definitely areas in my life that need improvement. It took me a minute to get with this concept because when I would look at myself, I didn't always like what I saw. Once I accepted the challenge to look at myself – not anyone else, but Yvette – it was not difficult to seek God on how to either bring positivity in that area or rid myself of those stumbling blocks.

Using this process helps me to think differently, which ultimately leads me to act differently. When God brings me to the other side of that challenge, I experience that sense of thrill of having obtained a victory and will be quick to plan a form of a mini-celebration of my accomplishment. Trust me when I tell you, the victory is often short-lived because when I least expect it, I am challenged with another area of my life that needs improvement.

Just when I thought I was in clear I find that there is more work for me to do on myself. If I was perfect, then I wouldn't need God; He's the only Perfect One that I know!

The work of self is never done!

Follow the Instructions

I once went shopping for a new desk. When I found the desk I wanted, I took a good look at and figured that it would be simple to assembler – after all it was just a few nuts and bolts, I had the tools to get it done, so it shouldn't be a big deal. When I was at home unpacking the desk pieces, I unpacked the written instructions. "I don't need these," I said to myself, tossed the instructions off to the side, and continued unpacking the desk pieces.

Before I knew it, almost an hour had passed and I still was not finished with putting the desk together. I became frustrated and baffled. My plan was not working! Why was something so simple getting to be so complicated? My goodness, it was only a desk with a few nuts and bolts – what is the problem?

I quickly figured out that I was the problem, or better yet, my thinking was the problem. I was attempting to do something that I had never done before. I had cut myself off from getting the needed knowledge to put the desk together when I tossed the instructions to the side as if I didn't need them. Once I read and followed the instructions, I had the desk assembled within minutes.

Striving to live a spiritual life conducive to God's will is following the written instructions outlined in His Word. Just like assembling that desk, the Word of God works the same way in my life – not only do I need to read His instructions, but I have to apply those instructions in all areas of my life. My human instincts get in the way from time to time because I don't always follow instructions but God's grace and mercy gives me another chance to become willing to follow and apply the instructions.

*Following instructions
makes life simple!*

Prayer is Not Magical

"Now I lay me down to sleep;
I pray the Lord my soul to keep.
If I should die before I wake,
I pray the Lord my soul to take."
(author unknown)

As a little girl, that was the first prayer that I learned. As far back as I can remember, I said that prayer EVERY NIGHT before I went to bed.

I remember hearing the adults say, "Just pray about it and God will work it out." As a child, I believed that whatever you wanted, all you had to do was "just pray about it" and God would make it happen. I also prayed to get old enough to pray to God for what I wanted to see what He would do.

I used to pray for God to bring my mama and daddy back together so they don't have to be divorced anymore. I got angry at God when that didn't happen because I thought whatever you wanted to happen was supposed to happen when you prayed about it.

For years, I harbored resentments about prayer because it seemed to me that God was not cooperating with me like He was with other people. Of course, back then, the only time that I prayed was for the matter of convenience. Whenever I wanted something or when my behind was on fire and I needed a quick way out of a situation, I had no problem with praying. Well, when God was not doing the things that I was asking Him to do, I drew a conclusion that you had to be one of God's "selective saints" to get your prayers answered and I was not one of them. When I would hear people talk about "God is good all the time," and "Oh, God has truly blessed me," I wanted to scream out, "SHUT UP!!!"

Eventually, I found out that I was going about prayer all the wrong way. I was looking at God to respond to my every wish and command like He is some kind of great magician that was supposed to make all my desires come true. God does not ride on a magic carpet, carry a magic wand in his hand, nor does he make people disappear into thin air! We are to pray with to God with thanksgiving and trust that things will be carried out according to His will and not my wishes.

I still pray for specific things, but today I know that God is the Ultimate Authority and He answers prayers that are conducive to His will, which means that things won't always turn out the way that I expect them to. My life is simpler when I accept God's will and move on to the next thing.

God does not own
a magic wand!

Too Tight

One of my favorite childhood adventures was shopping with my grandmother. One of the main reasons I loved going shopping with her was because she would buy me clothes, shoes, and anything that I wanted and asked her for.

Out of all that my grandmother would buy for me, I loved getting a new pair of shoes but I never got to wear them as long as I wanted to because the day came that either the shoes had become too small or too tight, which made my feet hurt on both accounts. "Well, baby, you've outgrown them and it's time for some new ones," my grandmother would say. Outgrowing a pair of shoes stopped being an issue when I became an adult (thank God!); nonetheless, I have another growth process to focus on each and every day – my spiritual growth.

Spiritual growth has its benefits; however, it's not always an easy process. Some things are easy to grasp; then there are others that truly bear "growing pains." Growing pains bring forth change, which is not always easy, but necessary nonetheless. As uncomfortable as change can sometimes be, it allows me to move past those familiar places that proved to be uncomfortable and not for my greater good. I don't have all the answers when it comes to spiritual growth but I have learned a few things along the way.

There are people, places, and situations that are no different to that pair of shoes that I had outgrown in my youth. Either I no longer fit in or if I tried to force myself to fit in, things would be so tight there is no room for me to move or to grow. Let's face it; being in a tight situation can also be hurtful!

Spiritual growth continues to bring into new

territory. After all, spent most of my life trying to fit in but today God allows me to focus more on what fits me for the greater good!

Why keep trying to squeeze into a place that I have outgrown?

No More Fighting

I have a past. I know that I am not the only person that has a past, but I know for a fact that I have a past! I wish I could say that all of my past has been pleasant but that would be untrue. Although it hasn't been all bad, I have had experiences that have been way past unpleasant. As a matter of fact, some things and have been dark and downright ugly.

I have experienced things in my past that caused tremendous harm to me and to those who cared about me. My actions got so ugly that it's only by God's grace that I didn't lose my life or my freedom. Trust me, I understand the songwriter's words, "Amazing grace, how sweet the sound, that saved a wretch like me!" That saving grace has allowed me to create a new life that consists of focusing forward rather than living in the past.

Again, I don't have to live in the past, but I do have to refer back to it from time to time. When I make those references of the past, it is not about what I did to save my life. I didn't have the power needed to save me. Only God could relieve me of my dark past. His grace gave me the courage to face my past, accept my past, ask for forgiveness, and to begin a new life's journey.

Accepting my past is not always easy for me and I know that it's not easy for those that I affected. There are those that remind me of my past every chance they get. Sometimes, their reminders are so intense that it appears that the events took place in recent times, which always led to endless arguments. I asked God how to deal with all of this, and He showed me that I don't have to allow people to keep me in the same bondage that He has delivered me from.

I had to separate myself from some people, including family members, but I just refused to fight anymore.

> *Fighting about yesterday*
> *will forfeit my future!*

Break Free

One of the first things I learned on the elementary school playgrounds was how to keep a secret. My classmates would ask, "Can you keep a secret?" One of my classmates would tell me something and I wasn't supposed to tell it to anyone else, no matter how bad I wanted to tell it. Sometimes I kept the secret and then sometimes I would tell that secret to another classmate.

Keeping secrets back in my childhood days was innocent fun, but as I got older, I began keeping secrets that could have been harmful to me and to other people. I worked very hard in trying to keep a secret about the activities that I was involved in during a dark period in my life.

Needless to say, those secrets weighed me down and the pain was so great that I arrived at the point of being too scared to live and too scared to die.

"A person is as sick as their secrets," a good friend told me. She helped me realize that all those years I kept those secrets I had emotionally imprisoned myself which was similar to my body being locked away in a prison cell. At this point, I was desperate to have peace and serenity but didn't have a clue that holding those secrets was blocking the path. I was sick, I was tired, and I was sick and tired of being sick and tired! My friend encouraged me to take a spiritual course of action to relieve myself, and I haven't held myself in that kind of imprisonment since.

Today I don't keep secrets but I continue to learn the practice of discretion and sharing in confidence. If something begins to eat away at my mind and spirit, I pray about it and then I share it with someone. Those two simple steps enable me from going back into that prison cell that I had built and confined myself in for so many years. Now I know what's like to experience peace and serenity in my life.

> *I hold the power to break free*
> *from my own prison!*

Great Accomplishments

During my school years, I was active in extra-curricular activities that were offered at school and the neighborhood community centers. I learned ballet, basketball, track & field, guitar, crocheting & knitting, pottery, karate, and a number of other things. I also enjoyed the competition that went along with these things, especially when I brought home certificates, plaques, and trophies from winning first, second, or third place.

I was fascinated about the different awards and recognitions that I had received. I loved having that sense of accomplishment, especially when I could gaze at the awards that symbolized those accomplishments.

Whenever I did what my parents asked me to do, I looked for some kind of award. After all, I did what I was asked to do at that moment. I remember asking my mother give me an award for something that I did, and she told me that my award was in heaven. I wasn't trying to hear that! I was a teenager that wanted what I wanted. Little I knew that analogy would become crystal-clear to me years later.

It is not necessary to have a plaque, certificate, or trophy every time that I do something that is of good nature and character. As a Christian, it's about doing the right thing to the best of my ability. Sometimes I don't do what's right or know what's right to do, but I focus forward on my journey.

It's not necessary to get a "pat on the back" for every good accomplishment. Most things that I do are the things that I am supposed to be doing anyway! I realized that my greatest accomplishment has been accepting Jesus Christ as my Lord and Savior which gives me a chance to receive that "award in heaven" that my mother had referred to.

What's your greatest accomplishment?

Yvette Wilson Bentley

About the Author

A native of Louisville, KY, Yvette Wilson Bentley has always enjoyed creative writing but it wasn't until recent years that she decided to pursue an active career as an author. ENHANCING THE JOURNEY was Yvette's freshman publication in early 2012. Yvette quickly became an avid learner and embraced each component of the publishing process from start to finish which has solidified her foundation as an author as well as a literary entrepreneur.

Yvette founded her own publishing company, *Wryte Type Publishing* in 2014 and is scheduled to print her first publication, "Thirst No More: A Woman's Journey to Restoration" in early 2015.

Yvette holds memberships in The Sisters of

Ruth Book Club and the M-Pact Writers Group. She has been a contributing writer for numerous newsletters and local magazines. She has also been a featured guest on a number of internet radio shows, including "Inspirational Talk With Toneal," "Awakened Internet Radio" and "Jerry Royce Live!"

Yvette also hosts a monthly talk-show, "Candid Conversations," where she headlines a variety of self-help topics and engages both a guest and her audience in transparent conversations. In addition, Yvette is a public speaker, workshop facilitator and life coach who has a passion for connecting with women that are seeking restoration in their lives from past and current life and spiritual issues.

In her spare time, Yvette enjoys reading, bowling, traveling and relaxing with friends and extended family members.

CONTACT INFORMATION

For more information, order additional books, to schedule speaking engagements, teleseminars, webinars, book club or group meetings:

Visit the website:
www.ywilsonbentley.com
Email us:
info@ywilsonbentley.com

Find me on Facebook:
www.facebook.com/YvetteWilsonBentley

Visit my blog:
www.ywilsonbentley.com/thejourney

Come "tweet" with me on Twitter
https://twitter.com/ynb65

PRODUCTION TEAM

Cover Art & Design:

Lloyd DeBerry

Fine Art & Graphics

www.fineartsandgraphics.com

Editing, Typesetting & Formatting:

Yvette Wilson Bentley

Wryte Type Publishing, LLC

www.wrytetype.com

www.ingramcontent.com/pod-product-compliance
Lightning Source LLC
Chambersburg PA
CBHW072051290426
44110CB00014B/1633